SERMON OUTLINES
for

Expository Preaching

Charles R. Wood

PUBLICATIONS

Grand Rapids, MI 49501

Sermon Outlines for Expository Preaching

Published by Kregel Publications, a division of Kregel, Inc., P.O. Box 2607, Grand Rapids, MI 49501. Kregel Publications provides trusted, biblical publications for Christian growth and service. Your comments and suggestions are valued.

For more information about Kregel Publications, visit our web site at: www.kregel.com

Cover design: Frank Gutbrod

Library of Congress Cataloging-in-Publication
Sermon outlines for expository preaching / by Charles R. Wood.
        p.   cm.
1. Bible—Sermons—Outlines, syllabi, etc. 2. Sermons—Outlines, syllabi, etc. I. Title. II. Charles R. Wood.
BS491.5.W66   1998   97-42133
251'.02—dc21

ISBN 0-8254-4121-8

2 3 4 5 / 04 03 02

Printed in the United States of America

Introduction

Many of the best modern pulpit communicators maintain that expository preaching is not just the best way to proclaim God's Word, but actually the only legitimate way to do so. Without entering the debate on preaching methodology, the experience of the compiler of this book of sermon outlines is that the expository approach is the best means of transferring the truth of God's Word from the pages of a book to the concourse of daily living.

Many of the stories and outstanding passages of Scripture, however, unfold like the buds of a flower under the exegetical study necessary for preaching expository messages. In the course of preparation for a message on a specific passage, story, or character, it is not uncommon for a number of other messages to suggest themselves or even to unfold in some detail during the preparation process.

The climate of our day appears to be one of distracted focus and limited attention. Congregations who once gladly listened to long-term series of expositional messages—some such series lasting a year or more—now seem loath to follow the same train of thought or contextual development for more than a very few weeks.

The sermons contained in this book are designed to provide for fuller treatment of subjects without protracted extension of that treatment. Congregations may not be willing to give attention to extended series of sermons, but they appear eager to embrace "short series" that extend for no more than a few weeks.

The four subjects covered in this book are treated in no less than four and no more than nine sermons, and the length of each series appears well suited both to the material to be covered and to the restless tenor of the day. Obviously, these sermons may be preached individually rather than in series form.

Each of these sermons has been preached by the compiler of this book from the pulpit of the local church of which he is pastor. Each series was well received, and attendances at the services when they were preached indicated that good reception.

These messages are basically expository in nature. They will be best presented after some careful study of the passage using the outline as a study guide. Consultation of a good Bible commentary will also prove helpful as the preacher may be enabled to augment the truths developed through my study of the passage.

After more than forty years of ministering the Word of God in the context of the local church, it is my conviction that there is no greater work than that of preaching the Word of God to a church congregation on a regular basis. May God bless these efforts to the advancement of the cause of preaching and of the cause of His dear Son.

CHARLES R. WOOD

Contents

Our "Know-It-All" God

Psalm 139:1–6

Introduction:

We use "know-it-all" pejoratively, but it is a term ultimately true concerning God. David deals with the concept of omniscience here—the idea that God knows everything. Verse 1 expresses it ("you have searched me and known").

I. **The Extent of Omniscience**
    A. To our movements
        1. "My downsitting/uprising" (v. 2) ("when I sit/when I stand" NIV)
        2. "My path and my lying down" (v. 3) ("my going out" NIV)
        3. "All my ways" (v. 3)
    B. To our thoughts
        1. "Thou understandeth my thought afar off" (v. 2)
        2. Afar off—even when my thoughts are far off, before they are framed, even when still unknown to me
        3. Thoughts are springs of feelings, words, actions, character
    C. To our actions
        1. "And art acquainted with all my ways" (v. 3)
        2. "You are familiar with all my ways" (v. 3 NIV)
    D. To our words
        1. "For there is not a word in my tongue" (v. 4)
        2. "Before a word is on my tongue you know it completely" (v. 4 NIV)

II. **The Operation of Omniscience**
    A. Observation of the minute and unimportant
        1. When I sit down and when I stand up
        2. Includes even things unimportant to me
    B. Knowledge of thought and motive
        1. God knows what they have been, what they are now, what they will be, what they would have been
        2. God—and only God—knows what is behind our thoughts
    C. Investigation of our ways
        1. "Thou compassest" (v. 3) (to winnow, sift out; "you discern" NIV)

7

    2. God takes notice of every step we take
    3. "Going out and lying down" (NIV)—public/private life
  D. Estimation of our words
    1. "Before a word is on my tongue, you know it completely" (v. 4 NIV)
    2. Negative used to make positive stronger
    3. Includes all that I say, all that I have power to say, all that I am tempted to say
  E. Remembrance of the past; acquaintance with the future (v. 5)
    1. God has hemmed us in behind, recording our transgressions or blotting out our sins
    2. God has blocked us out before, foreknowing all our needs and providing for all of them
  F. Watchful scrutiny, careful examination: "And laid thine hand" (v. 5)
    1. Covers all of life
    2. Deals on a moment-by-moment basis

III. The Meaning of Omniscience

  A. Awe—should beget reverence (v. 6)
    1. Literally, "wonderful knowledge of the God away from me"
    2. We see the most of God when we recognize Him as incomprehensible
  B. Comfort
    1. This is the tenor of the entire Psalm
    2. Should give great encouragement; He knows all about it when no one else understands and even when you can't express it
  C. Caution
    1. Should make us careful
    2. Should condition all of life

Conclusion:
  "What a mighty God we serve."

Thou, God, Seest Me

Psalm 139:7–12

Introduction:

Most environmentalists are very religious, but their religion—pantheism—is tied in to their environmentalism. Pantheism is the idea that God is all and all is God. Some aspect of pantheism approach accuracy. God is "all" in many ways (knowing, seeing, powerful, etc.). The biggest difference with pantheism is that God is separate from His creation.

I. Interrogation (v. 7)
- A. Where can I flee from Thy spirit?
- B. Where can I go from Thy presence?
- C. In brief: Where can I go to get away from God?

II. Information (vv. 8–11)
- A. Not to the heights and the depths (v. 8)
  1. Heb.: "the heavens"—the highest places
  2. Heb.: "Spread my couch in the lowest places"
- B. Not to global extremes (v. 9)
  1. "The wings of the morning" points toward the east where morning appears
  2. "The uttermost parts of the sea"—refers to the sea to the west—points to the west
- C. Not to darkness (v. 11)
  1. Darkness will cover me in what I am doing
  2. It can mean: "darkness will come upon me"; depression, gloom, etc., will keep me from seeing

III. Indications—Three Aspects of Omnipresence
- A. God's abiding presence (v. 8)
  1. If I ascend—Thou art there!
  2. If I descend—Thou art there!
- B. God's continuing activity (v. 10) no matter where I go
  1. Your hand will guide (guidance); God always guides, even when we are away from Him
  2. Your hand will hold me (preservation); God always sustains or we would not continue to exist
- C. God's unlimited scrutiny (v. 12)
  1. Darkness is no limitation on His observation
  2. Darkness will not be dark; night will shine like day

IV. Implications
   A. You can't get away from God! Ask . . .
      1. Jonah—in rebellion
      2. Abraham—in deception
      3. David—in sin
      4. Achan—in disobedience
   B. You can't be away from God! Ask . . .
      1. Elijah—in despondency
      2. Daniel—in danger
      3. Disciples—in uncertainty
      4. Stephen—in death

Conclusion:

"Thou, God, seest me" is a comforting and a cautioning truth: comfort when the lights go out, when "darkness comes upon us"; caution when pursuing our own purposes, ignorant of or contrary to His.

Marvelous Are Thy Works
Psalm 139:13–18

Introduction:
This passage deals with the greatness of God, but it is not a detached fact; it is a practical reality for everyday life.

I. **The Message of the Passage**
   A. God created us (vv. 13–14)
      1. "Thou hast created my kidneys," the innermost being of the individual
      2. "Woven me in my mother's womb"; God not only made me but also assembled me as well
      3. "I am fearfully [in a way to incite awed fear] and wonderfully [differently as distinct from animals] made"
      4. "That my soul knoweth right well"—I am fully convinced of and greatly impressed by this
   B. God knows us (vv. 15–16)
      1. "My frame was not hidden from you"
         a. "When I was made in secret"; the privacy of the womb
         b. "And skillfully wrought"; speaks again of creation
         c. "In the lower parts . . ."; symbolic, parallel
      2. "Your eyes saw my substance being yet unformed" (NKJV)
         a. Before I was actually formed, you saw me
         b. Idea: you knew what I would be even before I was
      3. "And in Your book they were all written, The days fashioned for me, When as yet there were none of them" (NKJV)
         a. Italics show KJV translators had trouble here
         b. Idea: you knew my life before it came to be
   C. God cares for us (vv. 17–18)
      1. "How precious also are thy thoughts unto me"
      2. "How great is the sum of them"

II. **The Meaning of the Passage**
   A. It takes omniscience and makes it personal
      1. Things God knew about me

a. He knew me before birth (v. 15)
b. He knew me before conception (v. 16a)
c. He knew me as complete before I was (v. 16b)
2. God not only knows everything, He knows me
B. It introduces the concept of omnipotence
1. Speaks of creation of the human body
2. God's power is seen nowhere more than in the human body
C. It explains why we oppose "abortion on demand"
1. God is the giver of life; abortion on demand actually intrudes on God's sovereignty
2. Life actually begins before creation; abortion on demand literally takes a human life
3. Life is planned in advance; abortion on demand interferes with God's providence

III. The Motivation of the Passage
A. It calls forth praise (v. 14)
1. Statement of purpose
a. I will praise you
b. Because of the way I am made and because my inner man knows how wonderful His works really are
B. It engenders confidence (v. 18)
1. "When I awake, I am still with you" (NIV)
2. I can sleep with confidence; if I can sleep, I can do anything with confidence in His keeping power

Conclusion:
This passage is well expressed by combining two choruses:
"What a Mighty God We Serve"
"How Kind and Gracious Is the Lord."

Slay the Wicked and Search Me
Psalm 139:19–24

Introduction:

This is a great doctrinal Psalm. The last six verses present significant problems, which we can best decipher by asking four questions:

I. **Why Are Verses 19–22 Here?**
    A. Provide jolt in reading passage
        1. Verses 23–4 what would be expected
        2. These four unexpected
    B. Evidently reflection brings the wicked to mind
        1. Either those presently bothering him
        2. Or the idea that God in His omniscience must see so much wickedness
    C. Sudden insertion surely designed to get attention

II. **What Do These Verses Mean To Us?**
    A. What the passage actually says:
        1. "May you slay the wicked and may I be rid of them as well."
            a. Those that speak against God
            b. Those that blaspheme God
            c. Those that rebel against God
        2. "I hate the wicked"
            a. For what they had done to God, not to me
            b. Judicial rather than personal hatred (remember, David filled an office)
        3. "Hate with a perfect hatred"
            a. Hatred is perfect in sense of proper
            b. Based on right considerations
    B. New Testament perspective (Matt. 5)
        1. Six verses mention O.T. law and give Christ's interpretation
        2. "It has been said . . ." (NKJV): Christ gives new teaching that leads to "hate the sin, but love the sinner"

III. **Why Do We Need God's Examination?**
    A. The near context
        1. David has spoken of "perfect hatred"
        2. Declares willingness to be examined relative to that

B. The greater context
   1. Has spoken of God's omniscience and knows full extent of it
   2. Has already known God's scrutiny
   3. Throws himself open to God's examination (this is a very knowledgeable request)
C. We don't know ourselves; He does know us (cf. Ps. 19:12–13)
   1. "Search": investigate thoroughly
   2. "Try": subject to a test for genuineness

IV. What Do We Need Examined?
A. The heart—the innermost being
B. The thoughts
   1. "My anxieties"—NKJV
   2. Even the jumbled thoughts which spill over
C. "See if there be any wicked way [of pain] in me" (KJV)
   1. Any way that will lead to pain
   2. Idea is to ferret out what might cause trouble or pain
D. "Lead me in the way everlasting"
   1. The way that will always last
   2. The way that leads to everlasting life

Conclusion:
What shall we do with ourselves? Ask that God might search us. Seek to determine if there is any way in us that will result in pain (1 Cor. 11:31–32).

Individual Responsibility

Introduction:
We live in a day of irresponsibility. Believers get caught up in wrong thinking such as: "A man's character is revealed by the countenance of his wife." Is that statement true or false?

I. **The Concept Explained**
   A. Not as difficult (or demanding) as it appears
   B. As individuals we are responsible for our own attitudes, actions, and words

II. **The Concept Examined**
   A. Regarding the fall of man (Gen. 3:1-13)
      1. Appears that Adam is "dragged into" Eve's sin
      2. Appears he is held responsible for the act of another
      3. Actually strengthens this teaching—he was held responsible for yielding to Eve and for eating of the fruit itself
   B. Regarding the "countenance theory"
      1. Michal (2 Sam. 6:14–16)
         a. David was joyous in the Lord (and of good character at this point)
         b. Michal was of sour countenance (and wrong)
      2. Abigail (1 Sam. 25:2–3)
         a. Nabal was about as bad as bad could be
         b. Abigail's countenance was unaffected by him

III. **The Concept Exampled**
   A. Matt. 5:43–48
      1. Your treatment of others is unrelated to their treatment of you
      2. Another way of expressing the "golden rule" (Luke 6:31)
   B. 1 Sam. 13:8–14
      1. Saul was disobedient
      2. Tried to blame disobedience on people
      3. His claim was disallowed: he made a choice; they didn't force an issue
   C. John 14:15–17; 15:9–11
      1. Obedience the key to several things
      2. These things are freely offered to all

3. Everyone can obviously do what is necessary to get these things

IV. The Concept Experienced
   A. You are responsible to do right no matter what anyone else does
      1. Another person's wrong is never an excuse for your wrong
      2. This is one tough concept to practice in life
   B. No one can make you do anything (either wrong or right)
      1. You can always choose not to do so even if it involves death
      2. All our conscious actions involve choices and decisions
   C. You can do anything you should do
      1. There is no commandment you can't do
      2. There is no reason out of your past that relieves you of the obligation to do right

Conclusion:
All of this is so easy to teach and so difficult to practice. Better think through what you are presently doing. Better take time to think next time.

Personal Accountability

2 Corinthians 5:10

Introduction:

Successful spiritual living demands recognition of personal accountability. Without this concept, life is essentially out of control.

I. **The Identification of This Judgment**
   A. It is different from the great white throne (Rev. 20:11–15)
      1. Great white throne is for all people, this one for Christians only
      2. Great white throne is on basis of Lamb's Book of Life; book of life not seen here
      3. Great white throne results in heaven/hell distinction; not so here
   B. What it is not (Rom. 8:1)
      1. A judgment of sin—sin has been already taken care of by Him and can't be brought against us again
      2. A judgment of standing—we are accepted in the Beloved (Eph. 1:6) and there is nothing we can add to our standing
   C. What it is
      1. Related to Luke 19:11–27; Matt. 25:14–30
      2. Related to 1 Cor. 3:10–15

II. **The Issues of This Judgment**
   A. The criteria of judgment
      1. What we have done with what we have been given (pounds, talents, etc)
      2. Matters of character (rather than specifics, this may have to do with character issues in general)
   B. The manner of judgment—we will be fully revealed
      1. "Revealed" means exposed; with the cover torn off
      2. This is already true (Heb. 4:13) and will be true (1 Cor. 4:5)
   C. The outcome of this judgment
      1. We will "get back" what we have done
      2. We will enjoy rewards or suffer the lack of rewards

III. **The Implications of This Judgment**
   A. The use of our talents

1. We are given talents, gifts, etc., to be used
　　　2. We will be called into account for that use
　B. The development of our character
　　　1. Character is incredibly important
　　　2. This gives perspective to some of the "character developing" trials we experience in life
　C. The release of our vengeance
　　　1. The desire to get even (and any attempts to do so) declares unbelief
　　　2. God is able to settle scores, and He will do so!
　D. The submission of our wills—conformity to His will produces the greatest results

IV. The Impact of This Judgment

"To have the glorious hope of being transformed into the likeness of Christ at His appearing in no way absolves us of the responsibility for the manner in which we conduct ourselves now." —Philip E. Hughes
　A. Our incentives
　　　1. God knows now
　　　2. We will be exposed later
　　　3. Our reward/loss of reward will be based on our performance and character
　B. Our expectations
　　　1. The marriage supper of the Lamb
　　　2. Rewards: places of responsibility in His kingdom

Conclusion:

You can't have spiritual success without accountability. This verse points to our own ultimate accountability. How will you stand in that day?

The Scriptures

Introduction:
"No man ever knew spiritual success who had not first settled the issue of his relationship to the Word of God."

I. **The Authority of the Bible (2 Tim. 3:16–17)**
   A. Scripture is given by God
      1. It is given by "inspiration," i.e., God-breathed
      2. The Bible is a message from God
   B. Scripture is given for express purposes
      1. Doctrine: imparting knowledge, teaching, communicating
      2. Reproof: setting things straight, clearing things up
      3. Correction: showing the right way
      4. Instruction in righteousness: training, teaching of what is right, what is required
   C. Scripture has designed results
      1. "Perfect" (KJV) = complete
      2. Completely equipped for all good works
         a. We are created for good works
         b. We are required to do good works
         c. We are equipped for good works

II. **The Sufficiency of the Bible (2 Peter 1:3–4)**
"His divine power has given us everything we need for life and godliness through our knowledge of Him who called us by his own glory and goodness" (v. 3 NIV).
   A. We have been given all things:
      1. Pertaining to life in general
      2. Pertaining to godliness—things that please God
   B. These "all things" come through . . .
"Through these he has given us very great and precious promises, so that through them you may participate in the divine nature and escape the corruption in the world caused by evil desires" (v. 4 NIV).
      1. Knowing Him—as we come to know Him through His Word—we come to know all that we need to know
      2. Knowing His promises—great and precious promises—and the things He has promised

C. These "all things" are designed to:
    1. Make us demonstrate that we share in His nature; as we live life according to the Bible, we demonstrate to ourselves and others that we have divine nature
    2. Help us escape the corruption in the world

III. The Practicality of the Bible
A. "Folly in front of a mirror" (James 1:22–25)
    1. A man looks in a mirror, sees a major problem, goes his way and does nothing about it
    2. The Bible points out our errors so we can do something about them
B. "Folly in the construction trades" (Matt. 7:24–27)
    1. Final result in view in this story
    2. Only one has something left at the end—the man who lived the Word

Conclusion:
The successful Christian is a person of the Book.

Practical Reality

James 3:13–18

Introduction:

How can you tell if someone is spiritual?

Our usual answers: they talk a lot about spiritual things, pray much, witness all the time, go to church more often than others, read their Bibles a lot, have been Christians for a long time, etc.

The biblical answer is very different.

I. **A Definition (v. 13)**
   A. Knowledge + wisdom = spirituality
      1. These two aspects summarize the subject
      2. Knowledge minus wisdom = danger; wisdom minus knowledge = uninformed
   B. Who is spiritual?
      1. The one doing good works: "conversation" = manner of life
      2. The one doing good works in a right way: "Meekness" = humility

II. **A Denial (vv. 14–16)**
   A. You know you're not spiritual when:
      1. You show bitter envying (sharp zeal)
         a. "Envying" = zeal (to boil, roil up)
         b. "Bitter" = sharp, harsh (that which hurts another)
      2. You harbor strife (self-advancement) in your heart
         a. "Strife" (from a political word, "to put self forward")
         b. Putting self first (common today: "My way or the highway")
   B. Such things can't be spiritual because:
      1. They arise from different sources
         a. Earthly: what men do
         b. Sensual: the product of your old nature
         c. Devilish: it's sure they don't originate with God
      2. They produce different results: these things actually produce confusion and evil works

III. **A Demonstration (v. 17); Catch the real thing!**
   A. Pure—in the moral sense—has to do with heart as well as actions

21

B. Peaceable; peace-loving: someone who loves peace will seek it
C. Gentle; considerate: includes courtesy, kindness
D. Easy to be entreated; reasonable: someone who can be reasoned with
E. Full of mercy; compassionate: first an attitude of heart
F. Full of good fruits; compassionate acts: compassion is useless if it doesn't act
G. Without partiality; impartial: has to do with favoritism based on wrong criteria
H. Without hypocrisy; sincere: without a mask

IV. A Declaration (v. 18)
A. Difficult verse to interpret
B. Appears to say: "Genuine spirituality operates in the realm of peace and reaps a harvest of practical righteousness."

Conclusion:
"A spiritual man is not a mystical, angelic, other-worldly person with a halo about his head and a faraway look in his eyes. A spiritual man is a person who is good when he doesn't feel like being good; who is patient when he feels like being impatient; who smiles and keeps sweet and does not retaliate when he is lied about and reviled; who is cheerful when he feels like being downcast; who goes to church when he would like to loaf at home or go on a joyride; who keeps steadily and sweetly on the job of being a Christian when he really feels like just going out and slamming the door."

What you are speaks so loudly that I can't hear what you say.

A Ministry Mindset

Ephesians 4:16

Introduction:

The church—and especially the local church—is compared to the human body several times in the New Testament.

I. **The Principles in the Comparison (1 Cor. 12:12–26)**
   A. The body is a unity/diversity (vv. 12–14)
      1. Continued, strong emphasis on unity of the body
      2. Recognition of complexity equally important
   B. Every part of the body is needed (vv. 15–17)
      1. Tendency to say, "They can get along without me."
      2. Tendency to despise lesser parts, roles
   C. God is sovereign in placing parts in the body (vv. 18–20)
      1. God has placed parts in the body
      2. Must assume that each body has adequate parts
   D. No part of the body may despise any other part (vv. 21–23)
      1. Corinthians had tendency to look down on others
      2. If every part is essential, every part is honorable
   E. No part of the body is unimportant (v. 24)
      1. Every part has a function
      2. No function can be easily dismissed
   F. The full function of the body is critical (v. 25)
      1. Failure of function leads to schism
      2. Full function tends to loving care
   G. Suffering in one part of the body= suffering in all (v. 26)
      1. When one suffers, all suffer
      2. Has more implications than we like to admit

II. **The Purpose of the Comparison (Eph. 4:11–16)**
   A. Everything needed in the body is supplied; if there is something missing, it likely isn't needed
   B. Everything supplied in the body is needed; there is actually no one without whom we can function
   C. Everyone has a function in the body; no one is excused from function
   D. Failure of function creates problems—problems for the individual and for the church
   E. Function outside designed function creates problems—it creates conflict
   F. Full function leads to body health; a healthy church is

one where all are functioning
G. Lack of growth indicates failure of function; the failure of body parts is just as likely to cause problems

III. The Practice in the Comparison (Romans 12:3–8)
  A. We need a proper self-evaluation (v. 3)
    1. We must not think of ourselves more highly than the body
    2. We must be capable of doing what we should
  B. We need a proper group relationship (vv. 4–5)
    1. Need to look at our gifts
    2. Need to look at our "fit" in the body
  C. We need a proper approach to practice (vv. 6–8)
    1. Need to know what we can do
    2. Need to get busy doing it

Conclusion:
Question: Are you fulfilling your function? In the immortal words of the Nike ads: "Just do it!"

Spirit Empowerment
Ephesians 5:18–21

Introduction:
Most of us would like to know the power of God on our lives—and on our ministries. Paul provides the secret of power, and it is much simpler than we have often been led to believe. It is revealed in Ephesians 5:18: "Be not drunk with wine . . . but be filled with the Spirit" (KJV).

I.   **A Commandment—"Keep on being filled with the Spirit"**
  A. This is a continual matter
  B. Appears to be something well within the reach of every Christian

II. **A Contrast—"Do not be filled with wine, wherein is excess"**
  A. Wine is external influence; so is spirit
  B. Wine controls; Holy Spirit controls
  C. Wine leads to excesses; Holy Spirit does not

III. **A Confusion**
  A. We are filled by praying—actually, prayer for filling may be misguided
  B. We are filled by experiencing—it may or may not involve an experience
  C. We are filled by emptying of self—don't really know how you go about doing that
  D. We are filled by claiming by faith—should we claim by faith what we are commanded to do?

IV. **Some Conditions**
  A. The fruit of the Spirit (Gal. 5:22ff.)
    1. All internal matters of spirit and attitude
    2. These things should characterize every child of God
    3. How can we lay claim to the fullness of the Spirit when the presence of the Spirit is not even being demonstrated
  B. Grieve not the Spirit (Eph. 4:30ff.) (It doesn't take something extreme to grieve the Spirit; He is very sensitive.)
    1. Bitterness: Most of us can interpret this by experience

2. Wrath: feeling of antagonism that is expressed
3. Clamor: settled indignation, internal animosity
4. Evil speaking: slander, abusive, harmful speech (whether to or about someone else)
5. Malice: inclination of mind that takes pleasure in the hurt of another
6. Kindness: Spirit-imparted goodness of heart
7. Tenderheartedness: a heart that is easily moved or touched
8. Forgiveness: "freely, generously, wholeheartedly, spontaneously, eagerly"

C. Quench not the Spirit (1 Thess. 5:19 KJV)
1. "Quench": extinguish light or fire
2. Don't throw cold water on what the Spirit may be doing

V. The Conclusions—Results of Fullness of the Spirit

A. Personal (v. 19): an overflowing, joyful spirit within
B. Spiritual (v. 20): a perpetual spirit of thanksgiving that recognizes the hand of God in every circumstance of life
C. Relational (v. 21): an attitude toward each other that places the other first, a yielding spirit
D. Ministerial (Acts 4:31): connected with boldness in communicating the Word

Conclusion:

"Be filled with the Spirit."

Pretty complicated? Not at all!

"We could greatly simplify spiritual things if we would only seriously practice the simple truths of Scripture."

Spiritual Relationships

Introduction:
God's people are called upon to live life relationally. All of life involves relationships—unless you live in a cave. Three relationships are critical to spiritual success.

I.   **A Relationship to God (Acts 4:13)**
    A.   The character of the disciples
        1.   "Boldness": courage to take on the experts
        2.   "Ignorant and unlearned": without formal training, merely common men
    B.   The experience of the disciples
        1.   They had been with Jesus—a critical point; they were discipled
        2.   Being with Jesus had changed them—as it always will
        3.   The changes that were made were visible—they should be
        4.   The changes that were made had an impact—they will
    C.   A private presence that produces visible results
        1.   Doing something you are not capable of doing
        2.   Doing something contrary to the person you are
        3.   Doing something obviously supernatural

II.   **A Relationship to Fellow Believers (John 13:34–35)**
    A.   In the words of Christ
        1.   The context: concerned with perpetuation (no doubt part of His concern with love for each other)
        2.   The commandment: a "new" commandment—new in the sense of fresh
        3.   The comparison: in the same way that I have loved you (part of newness)
        4.   The consequence: becomes a matter of testimony
    B.   Developing a love that shows—this is a love for others

III. **A Relationship to the Unconverted World (2 Cor. 5:14–15)**
    A.   A call to:
        1.   Live life deliberately; the whole pitch of this section is toward rational thought
        2.   Live life submissively; live as "unto" Him

3. Live life vicariously; we live "in His place"
4. Live life redemptively; the context demands interest in salvation of others
B. Living life to win others to Him
   1. A goal of every life should be the salvation of others
   2. How much thought do you give to this?

Conclusion:

"No man is an island; no man can stand alone."

We are constantly faced by relationships: a proper relationship to Him, a proper relationship to other believers, a proper concern for a lost world.

Love Thy Neighbor
Leviticus 19:9–18

Introduction:

Jesus said ". . .Thou shalt love the Lord thy God with all thy heart . . . soul . . . and mind. This is the first and great commandment. And the second is like unto it, Thou shalt love thy neighbor as thyself" (Matt. 22:37–39 KJV).

But how can I love my neighbor? Oddly enough, an Old Testament passage provides some of the best information in the Bible. According to this passage, I can love my neighbors by:

I. Making Provision for Their Needs (vv. 9–10)
  A. This involves a mind-set, a way of thinking
  B. Note: no command to give, just to provide for them

II. Practicing Integrity in All My Relations (v. 11)
  A. Encompasses lying, cheating, stealing
  B. Lack of integrity = lack of love; I love myself more than another person and show it in this way

III. Refraining from Invoking God's Name on Someone (v. 12)
  A. More here than taking God's name in vain
  B. Involves invoking the will of God on someone else

IV. Keeping My Commitments (v. 13)
  A. I must treat my neighbor justly and equitably
  B. I will pay a fair wage and do so promptly
  C. No one can grow rich at the expense of another and claim to love

V. Showing Care if My Neighbor Is Less Fortunate Than I (v. 14)
  A. Has to do with proper assistance/provision for handicapped
  B. Can extend to not making fun of anyone's discomfiture

VI. Treating All as Equal to Me and to All Others (v. 15)
  A. Everyone is to be viewed as of equal worth
  B. Note: neither the poor nor rich are to be preferred just because either are poor or rich

VII. Speaking Truthfully of My Neighbor (v. 16)
  A. Love is truthful, but seeks to focus on good
  B. Love never needlessly brings harm to a neighbor

C.   Rules out any form of character assassination

VIII. Rejecting Hateful Thoughts Toward Another (v. 17a)
A.   Hatred is the opposite of love
B.   Thinking hateful thoughts is dangerous as it can result in hateful actions (we rarely act without prior thought)

IX.   Rebuking Someone When Wrong (v. 17b)
A.   Forgotten aspect of love; love rebukes wrong
B.   Purpose of rebuke is to keep individual from suffering sin
C.   Rebuke would be much easier if we developed a spirit that could accept it (problem of lack of maturity)

X.   Refusing to Entertain Wrong Desires (v. 18)
A.   Deals with grudges and thoughts of revenge
B.   Love rules out even wrong desires for another's ill-being
C.   The flip side: a disposition to do good

Conclusion:

"Ministry takes place when divine resources meet human needs through loving channels to the glory of God."

—Warren Wiersbe

"I've Got the Joy . . ."

Introduction:

We used to sing a little chorus: "I've Got the Joy, Joy, Joy . . ."

Watching many Christians makes me wonder why there seems to be so little joy among God's people. We seem to have everything figured out except how to be joyful. Joy is a fruit of the Spirit, something we should be developing.

I. **You Know You Haven't Got the Joy When:**
   A. You are constantly complaining
   B. You often withdraw from spiritual life (or life in general)
   C. You are frequently angry
   D. You sense constant frustration
   E. You are seldom grateful

II. **You Haven't Got the Joy Because You Lost It to:**
   A. Your own self
      1. Self-centeredness is incredibly common
      2. Self-centeredness (in all its forms) is the enemy of joy
   B. A focus on circumstances
      1. Biblical joy is unrelated to circumstances—Paul is proof
      2. A focus on circumstances limits joy to "the good times"
   C. General negativity
      1. The child of God always has reason to be positive
      2. Negativity is dishonoring to the Lord
   D. A spirit of rebellion
      1. A rebellious child is never a happy one
      2. Rebellion is a rejection of God's rule
   E. Concern with happiness
      1. Happiness is often the enemy of joy
      2. Joy is critical; happiness is not
   F. Basic disobedience
      1. Obedience is the pathway to joy
      2. A disobedient spirit is always joyless

III. **You Are Likely Substituting for Joy:**
   A. Happiness

    B. Mindlessness
    C. Activity
    D. Acquisition
    E. Relationships

IV. If You Really Want Joy, It Comes From (John 15:11):

    A. God's pruning (v. 2)
    B. Progressive holiness (v. 3)
    C. Abiding in Him (vv. 4, 6, 7)
    D. Exposure to Scripture (v. 3)
    E. Answers to prayer (v. 7)
    F. A sense of God's love (v. 9)
    G. Basic obedience (v. 10)
    H. Real fruit bearing (v. 8)

Conclusion:

The fruit of the Spirit is *joy*. Joy is developed as we grasp the things recorded in this passage. As His joy remains in us, our joy will be full.

Her Name Was Grace Irene

Introduction:

What a lovely name! Grace Irene. It is especially beautiful if it is spiritually motivated. Grace refers to God's favor where punishment is deserved. Irene is the Greek word for peace. Peace is a very important concept in the New Testament, with the word itself used more than one hundred times.

I.   **Peace Is a Gift from God (John 14:27)**
  A. It is donated—a gift from the hand of God
  B. It is divine; it is *His* peace (all real peace belongs to Him)
  C. It is different—different from any peace that the world can give (source, duration, depth, character, etc.)
  D. It is desirable; it will keep your heart and mind

II. **Peace With God Is the Basis for All Peace**
  A. The problem of peace (Eph. 2:14–17)
      1. We are naturally at enmity with God (opposite of peace not necessarily war)
      2. There is a distance between us and God
  B. The provision of peace (Rom. 5:1)
      1. Peace with God comes through His finished work on Calvary
      2. God provided the possibility of peace
  C. The person of peace (Col. 1:20)
      1. Peace is actually in Christ
      2. Only the person in Christ can know peace

III. **Peace Is Internal (Phil. 4:6–7; Col. 3:15)**
  A. The source of peace takes us back to God/Christ
  B. The securing of peace
      1. Prayer
      2. Thanksgiving
  C. The security of peace
      1. Shall *keep* your hearts and minds
      2. Let it *rule*

IV. **Peace Is External**
  A. It is commanded (1 Thess. 5:13); God views peace among His people as important

B. It is challenged (Heb. 12:14); we are to "pursue" rather than merely "follow after"
C. It is conditioned (Rom. 12:18); our responsibility is to do all we can to create and maintain peace
D. It is commended (2 Cor. 13:11)

V. Peace Is a Project (Matt. 5:9)

A. The role—a peacemaker is just that—someone who makes peace between people (saved and unsaved)
B. The reward—"Blessed"; happy is a sense of having acted in the manner of Christ and God
C. The recognition: they shall be called—known as—the children of God. Peace should be a distinguishing characteristic of the child of God.

Conclusion:

Peace and peacefulness should characterize God's people.

"It is one thing for us to go to heaven and quite something else for heaven to come to us. There is a deeper fellowship with the Son and the Father for those who love Him, seek Him, and obey Him. We experience His peace as we communicate with the Father and the Son in love."

—Warren Wiersbe

Longsuffering

Galatians 5:22

Introduction:

Longsuffering is mentioned about fifteen times in the New Testament and is very important. It is particularly important because it is a characteristic of God. "He could have called ten thousand angels to destroy the world and set Him free," but instead, He demonstrated longsuffering.

I. **Longsuffering Defined**
   A. A combination of words that mean "long" and "temper"
      1. Long in sense of prolonged, continued
      2. Temper refers to any demonstration of emotion
   B. Longsuffering: self-restraint that does not hastily retaliate or promptly punish in the face of provocation; it is the opposite of anger, associated with mercy, and attributed to God
   C. Putting up with a lot from people over a long period of time

II. **Longsuffering in God**
   A. It demonstrates His mercy and grace (Rom. 9:22; 1 Tim 1:16)
      1. Mercy is not getting what we deserve
      2. Grace is getting what we do not deserve
   B. It stays His judgment (1 Pet. 3:20; 2 Pet. 3:9)
      1. Situation with Noah (1 Pet. 3:20)
      2. Prolongs for the sake of ungodly men
   C. It allows for salvation (Rom. 2:4; 2 Pet. 3:15)
      1. Were it not for longsuffering, no one would be saved
      2. Longsuffering allows time for men to come to God on their own

III. **Longsuffering in Christians**
   A. It is essential to total Christianity (2 Cor. 6:1–10)
      1. ". . . that ye receive not the grace of God in vain" (KJV)
      2. The grace of God is designed to produce certain things in us—longsuffering is one of them
   B. It is a mark of Christian testimony (Eph. 4:2; 2 Tim. 3:10)
      1. ". . . walk worthy of the vocation wherewith ye are called"

35

    2. We look in the wrong places for testimony—at what men do rather than at what they are
- C. It is a result of internal strength (Col. 1:11)
  1. We are strengthened by the work of the Holy Spirit
  2. Such strengthening produces longsuffering
- D. It is part of a "designer wardrobe" (Col. 3:12)
  1. It is among the things we are to put on as Christians
  2. It is part of God's design for every life
- E. It is necessary for a fruitful ministry (2 Tim. 4:2)
  1. It relates to the things a minister is to do as part of his calling
  2. It is necessary because people won't accept reproof, rebuke, etc.
- F. It is required to secure a reward (Heb. 6:12; James 5:10)
  1. Without longsuffering one won't hang in long enough to receive the reward that God intends
  2. Job's longsuffering was demonstrated in his handling of his friends

Conclusion:

The Holy Spirit produces this fruit. It is a fruit often rendered patience, but it is not. The indwelling Spirit makes us longsuffering—if we allow His work!

A Christian Gentleman
Galatians 5:22

Introduction:

What adjectives do you think of when you hear the names Bill Clinton, Mike Tyson, Abraham Lincoln, Billy Graham? What adjectives do you think of with your mate, children, parents, employer, fellow-workers, neighbors? What adjectives do people think of when they think of you?

"Gentleness" can best be rendered by "kindness" in modern parlance.

I. **The Concept Examined**
   A. Five words are used
      1. All from the same stem
      2. All have the same basic meaning
   B. Twenty uses in the New Testament
      1. Variety of translations
      2. All are in the same "family"
   C. Word moves from useful to making effective to kind
   D. William Tindal: gentleness = courtesy

II. **The Concept Explained: The Words Involved Draw Pictures**
   A. It is a perfect gentleman
      1. Someone with very good manners
      2. Someone who acts properly in every situation
   B. It is a lubricating oil
      1. That which eases friction
      2. That which seeks out friction and smooths it
   C. It is a mediator
      1. A person who brings two estranged parties together
      2. Someone who seeks the best interests of everyone involved

III. **The Concept Exampled**
   A. It is best seen in God
      1. Romans 2:4: basic word "goodness," used twice; goodness of God is designed to lead to repentance, referring to wicked (KJV)
      2. Titus 3:4: "kindness," used here refers to mankind in general, both saved and unsaved

    3. Ephesians 2:7: "kindness" toward the redeemed is almost a synonym for "grace"
  B. It is shown by the good Samaritan (Luke 10:30–37)
    1. He had no reason/requirement to get involved
    2. He went beyond the requirement
    3. He placed another's well-being above his own
  C. It is personified by Barnabas
    1. Acts 4:36–7: contributed to well-being of others
    2. Acts 15:36–41: handled division wisely
    3. 1 Cor. 9:6: reappears in Paul's life

IV. The Concept Expanded—Contemporary Parallels
  A. Synonyms: good natured, gentle, tender, affectionate, mild under provocation, goodness, benignity, calmness of spirit, given to seeking the happiness of everyone possible
  B. Antonyms: harsh, sour, morose, ill-tempered, severe, crabbed, unpleasant, rude, discourteous

V. The Concept Exhorted
  A. It should be our signature
    1. What constitutes spirituality?
    2. Introduces radically different concept of Christianity
  B. It should be our second-nature
    1. Should be natural response to pin-pricks
    2. Should be a dominating factor in our lives

Conclusion:
"[True] religion makes no one crabbed, and morose, and sour. [Spirituality] sweetens the temper, corrects the disposition, makes the heart kind, disposes us to make all around us as happy as possible."

Doin' Good

Galatians 5:22

Introduction:
The good life: lookin' good, feelin' good, talkin' good, havin' good(s), doin' good, bein' good. But are you biblically good?

I. **Goodness Arises Out of Righteousness**
   A. There is none good but God (Luke 18:19)
      1. Point: either Christ was God or not good
      2. Point: no man is good in this way of himself
   B. Goodness only comes from God (Rom. 4:1–8)
      1. Justification makes us as if we had never sinned
      2. It also provides us with imputed righteousness (He clears our account and makes a new deposit in it)

II. **Goodness Reflects the Goodness of God (2 Thess. 1:11)**
   A. God is generally good
      1. God's general dealings with men are good
      2. Most of God's dealings with us are good
   B. Because our focus is wrong, we miss God's goodness
      1. We focus on what's wrong (helped by media, etc.)
      2. We focus on what we do not get

III. **Goodness Approximates the Goodness of Christ**
   A. He went about doing good (Acts 10:38)
      1. His life and ministry were characterized by doing good
      2. Times of harshness, etc. were the exception
   B. He usually did good first (John 8:1–11)
      1. He often met physical/psychological needs first
      2. The spiritual sometimes almost appears appended

IV. **Goodness Reveals Itself in the Goodness of Life**
   A. We are to do good to . . .
      1. Other Christians (Gal. 6:10)
      2. All men (1 Thess. 5:15)
      3. Those who misuse us (Matt. 5:43–44)
   B. Those who have more are especially responsible (1 Tim. 6:17–18)
   C. A constant reminder (Heb. 13:16)

V. **Goodness Is Opposed by the Exaltation of Self**
   A. The problem:

1. Selfishness—thinks only of the well-being of self
2. Self-will—fails to recognize the rights/opinions of others (or even of the fact that others have a right to an opinion)
3. Self-conceit—thinks of self as above all others

B. The antidote (Phil. 1:27; 2:1–4)

Conclusion:

A man bearing the fruit of the Spirit must be characterized as good. A man who is not known as "good" has a poor testimony. Albert Barnes said it: "A Christian must be a good man."

". . . That a Man Be Found Faithful"

Galatians 5:22

Introduction:
Galatians 5:22 is dealing with traits of character produced in men by the Holy Spirit and made evident in inter-personal relationships. Hence "faithfulness" (NIV) is the preferred translation in this place.

I. **What Is Faithfulness?**
   A. An attribute of God—seen in Psalm 89
      1. Completely reliable
      2. Steadfastness toward His covenant people—even to the point of stubbornness
   B. A characteristic of men
      1. To fit meaning here—faithfulness
      2. Consistency: always meeting obligations, reliable

II. **Why Should I Be Faithful?**
   A. Because God is faithful
      1. One of His primary characteristics
      2. Sanctification seeks to restore God's image in us
   B. Because God rewards faithfulness (parable of the talents, "It is accounted in stewards . . .")
   C. Because life is lubricated by faithfulness
      1. Life is made more difficult by unfaithfulness
      2. All of life works better when men are dependable

III. **How Should I Demonstrate Faithfulness?**
   A. Faithfulness—based on God's faithfulness—is not:
      1. Emotional: based on swinging feelings; faithfulness is part of God's character
      2. Occasional: something that comes and goes; faithfulness is constant in God
      3. Peripheral: something that can be crowded out by circumstances; faithfulness is at the heart of God's character
      4. Conditional: based on the faithfulness of other people; God is faithful regardless of the performance of His people
      5. Passive: referring only to ground held and not faithfulness extended; God's faithfulness is active

41

      6. Permissive: unwilling to rebuke, etc.; God is as faithful to confront as He is to do any other thing
      7. Dependent: resting on things going well; God is faithful regardless of how things may be going

B. Faithfulness is
1. Keeping your promises
2. Honoring your marriage vows
3. Using your talents
4. Making the most of your time
5. Standing by your friends
6. Managing your money
7. Doing your best work
8. Committing to a local church

Conclusion:

"The Christian is faithful as a man; faithful as a neighbor, friend, father, husband, son. . . . All pretensions of being under the influence of the Spirit, when such fidelity does not exist, are deceitful and vain."

—Albert Barnes

Meekness

Galatians 5:23

Introduction:
Biblical meekness is a close relative of humility. This is an almost unknown virtue.

I. **What Is Meekness?**
  A. It is not
    1. False modesty
    2. Spineless surrender
    3. Cowardly retreat
    4. Artificial humility
    5. Passive selfishness
  B. It is: acceptance of one's self as one really is in the sight of God; a proper view of one's self
    1. Basically an attitude (Gal. 6:1)
    2. An attitude toward God (Matt. 5:5)
    3. Arises from a proper understanding of self and God

II. **How Does Meekness Show?**
  A. In response to God's dealings (example: Moses)
    1. Listening to what God has to say
    2. Accepting God's will for life
    3. Submissive to the commandments of God
    4. Unmoved by the problems and trials that come in the course of God's will being revealed
  B. In response to others' dealings
    1. Aware that God uses others to work in our lives
    2. Open to others shaping our lives
  C. In the course of daily life
    1. Understanding, not demanding
    2. Gracious, not judgmental
    3. Tender without surrender
    4. Teachable, not unreachable
    5. An actor, not a reactor
    6. Respectful, not disrespectful

III. **How Is Meekness Developed?**
  A. Proper recognition
    1. How much I really need it
    2. Who I really am—many problems stem from a sense of self-importance

        3. What I really have
        4. What I got from God
   B. Created desire
        1. Not natural
        2. This only comes from exposure to the Word of God
   C. Clear application
        1. Ask for it
        2. Claim the power of the Holy Spirit
        3. Work on it at every possible point

Conclusion:

It is likely that no fruit of the Spirit runs more against the old nature!

Seven Steps to Self-Control

Galatians 5:23

Introduction:

Self-control: the ability to choose one's own thoughts, words, and actions and to put those choices into action. We know what it is. The problem lies in doing it. Here are seven practical steps to help in the process.

I. **Admit Your Problem**
    A. We do things because we choose them: "A man's temptation is due to the pull of his own inward desires, which greatly attract him" (James 1:14, paraphrased).
    B. We are hurt by rationalization
        1. We ignore problems
        2. We deny problems
        3. We explain away our problems
        4. We blame others for our problems

II. **Put Your Past Behind You (Phil. 3:13–14)**
    A. Past failures do not determine present potential
    B. A focus on past failures guarantees repetition

III. **Talk Back to Your Feelings**
    A. Do not allow your moods to manipulate you
        1. Many self-control problems are wrapped up in feelings that involve the physical
        2. God wants you to master your moods (Titus 2:11–12)
    B. God's grace gives us the power to do what is right

IV. **Believe You Can Change**
    A. Your beliefs determine your behavior
        1. Victory begins in your thought life
        2. You need real conviction of the correctness of Philippians 4:13
    B. Focus on God's power and promises

V. **Make Yourself Accountable**
    A. Find someone to share your burden
    B. Criteria for an "accountability partner:"
        1. Someone of the same sex
        2. Someone who will follow through on a commitment to you

        3. Someone who is confidential

        4. Someone who will confront you

VI. Avoid Temptation

  A. Don't give Satan an advantage: "Don't give the devil a chance " (Eph. 4:27, paraphrase).

    1. Think through your problem

    2. Plan in advance

  B. Make necessary changes

    1. May require major environmental changes

    2. May require relational changes

VII. Depend on Christ's Power

  A. Be sure of proper sequence: Spirit control comes first (Gal. 5:16)

  B. Understand what you already possess (Phil. 2:13; 4:13)

Conclusion:

There is no magic formula for self-control. Self-control is much easier for some. Self-control is required of all. "The secret of self-control is Christ's control."

Biblical Addition

2 Peter 1:1-9

Introduction:
Addition is the easiest part of math—the beginning. Second Peter 1:5–7 forges a chain, no link of which may be broken.

I. **The Background**
    A. The gifts of God
        1. We have been given all things
        2. We have been given precious promises
    B. The scope of those gifts
        1. For all of secular life
        2. For all of spiritual life
    C. The source of those gifts: the Word of God
    D. The purpose of those gifts
        1. That we might have the divine nature
        2. That we might escape the world's corruption

II. **The Basics**
    A. How does verse 5 relate to the rest of the passage?
        1. Deals with His part and ours
        2. It is the logical conclusion of the previous section
    B. Because of what He has done for us:
        1. We should add some qualities to our spiritual life
        2. We should do so with diligence (careful attention)

III. **The Basis—Faith—Five Pertinent Aspects of Faith**
    A. A body of beliefs (Acts 6:7; 16:5; Rom. 1:5)
        1. Almost always has "the" before it
        2. We would say "the Christian faith"
    B. An acceptance of, dependence on those beliefs (Rom. 1:17)
        1. This is what we call "saving faith"
        2. It is actually a mental activity
    C. Accepting something as true even though it cannot be seen or proved (Heb. 11:1–3; Rom 14:22–23)
    D. Belief that something will happen because God said so (Rom. 12:3; Eph. 6:16; 1 Tim. 1:4)
        1. A vital issue in prayer
        2. Relates to a special ability to expect and secure things from God (1 Cor. 12:9; 13:2)

E. Enough confidence in God to enable me to obey Him (Heb. 11)
   1. This is "obedient faith"
   2. Important to the rest of the column that is to be added

IV. The Benefits
A. It will keep one from barrenness
   1. Barrenness means to be without fruit
   2. Fruit in general—mentioned often in Scripture
B. It will keep one from blindness
   1. Inability to have perspective
   2. Inability to recognize what has really happened

Conclusion:
The first two aspects of faith are already in place. The next three must be developed and are matters of choice. Faith: "the foundation that holds us and the engine that drives us."

"The Book of Virtues"

2 Peter 1:5

Introduction:
Former Secretary of Education William Bennet has written the book. It deals with all manner of character issues. Long before Bennet was invented, Peter made virtue an issue in the Christian life. What is virtue as it is used in this passage?

I. **Identifying the Meaning of "Virtue"**
- A. The word is used in four places (KJV):
  1. Philippians 4:8—note contrast with "praise"
  2. 1 Peter 2:9—use of "praises" likely not accurate
  3. 2 Peter 1:3—attached to God
  4. 2 Peter 1:5
- B. It's basic meaning is excellence—difference between older and newer commentaries (older has idea of courage, strength, manliness)
- C. Fine tuned, it means moral excellence in this place

II. **Clarifying the Meaning of "Virtue"**
The "moral" of moral excellence has two meanings:
- A. Ethical morality
  1. The consistent application of Biblical principle to all of life
  2. Passages that have to do with . . .
     a. Interpersonal relationships
     b. Employer/employee relationships
     c. Personal integrity issues
     d. The manner of our work (don't forget "excellence")
  3. Example: Daniel
- B. Sexual morality
  1. The acceptance and practice of Biblical truth
  2. Passages that have to do with . . .
     a. Marriage
     b. Sex outside marriage
     c. Thought life
  3. Example: Joseph

III. **Applying the Meaning of "Virtue"**
- A. A Christian should excel in character—this is the essence of a good testimony

B. A Christian should excel in moral conduct—this is the essence of personal holiness

Conclusion:

We are responsible to develop the character that wasn't developed in and for us. We are responsible to obey the Bible in regard to moral purity.

What Do You Know?

2 Peter 1:5

Introduction:
The knowledge spoken of here is more than merely acquiring facts: "This Christian knowledge sheds its light on all the facts and aims of life."

I. **What Is Knowledge?**
    A. The meaning of the word
        1. Different from knowledge in verses 3 and 8
        2. Involves a right understanding
        3. Includes the ability to tell the difference between two things
    B. A practical knowledge, discretion that leads to an increasing ability to discern

II. **How Does It Operate?**
    A. It tells the difference between right and wrong
    B. It tells the difference between good and bad teachers
    C. It tells the difference between important and unimportant; Satan is constantly trying to keep us focused on themes that don't really matter
    D. It tells the difference between edifying and derogatory
    E. It tells the difference between good, better, and best

III. **Why Do We Need It?**
    A. Because it is commanded; "Because I said so," is always sufficient coming from God
    B. Because it keeps us out of false doctrine; it is possible for solid believers to fall into this
    C. Because it keeps us from following false teachers; they are everywhere
    D. Because it keeps us from disillusionment in Christianity; following the false will always disillusion
    E. Because it helps us determine what to battle; many of the battles being fought today do not appear worth fighting (in the light of history, etc.)
    F. Because it keeps us from mediocrity in our spiritual lives—settling for the good instead of the better, etc.

IV. **How Do We Get It?**
    A. Recognize the context of life (Matt. 10:16)

B. Recognize the manner of life (Matt. 10:16)
C. Recognize the role of the Word (Heb. 4:12)
D. Immerse one's self in the Word (Heb. 5:14)
E. Examine every teacher and teaching (1 John 4:1)
F. Apply the simple test: Does this accord with the Word of God? Does this teacher follow Christ?

Conclusion:

Most "discernment criteria" are invalid. E.g.: Does it work? Are souls being saved? What's the attendance? How large are the offerings? How do I feel? The Bible is the test! We gain this kind of knowledge by dedication to the Word.

Control Yourself

2 Peter 1:5

Introduction:

Self-control: the ability to eat a single salted peanut or just one potato chip. Someone has said regarding Christians, "Those who wish to transform the world must be able to transform themselves."

I. **What Is Temperance?**
   A. From the word for power or lordship
   B. Comes to mean power or control over self—inner strength
   C. Opposite: lack of power or control
   D. The person who is mastered by the Lord and His will

II. **What Does Temperance Include?**
   A. Usually limited to matters of food, drink, and sex
   B. The ability to do what one chooses in spite of:
      1. Sensual temptations
      2. Outside criticism
      3. Accidents of circumstance
      4. Appeals to self-ease and self-service
      5. Enticements of praise and flattery
      6. Enemies' rage
   C. The guiding, directing, and controlling of *all* faculties and actions, the voluntary forgoing of privileges

III. **Why Is Temperance Important?**
   A. Because its possession is so helpful
      1. Kept Joseph out of trouble
      2. Prepared Daniel for a place of prominence
      3. Kept Paul on track in the face of great difficulties
   B. Because its absence is so damaging
      1. Caused Peter all kinds of problems
      2. Can result in disqualification (1 Cor. 9:27)
      3. Accounts for much Christian failure

IV. **How Is Temperance Gained?**
   A. Face your failures; we tend to be strong in rationalizations
   B. Forget the past; a focus on past failures guarantees repetition
   C. Resist your feelings; don't allow your moods to manipulate you (Titus 2:11–12)

53

D. Believe you can change; your beliefs determine your behavior
E. Make yourself accountable; find someone to share your burden
F. Avoid temptation; don't give Satan an advantage
G. Depend on Christ's power; recognize what you already possess

Conclusion:

There is no magic formula. Self-control is required—we are to develop it. "The secret of self-control is Christ's control."

Patience and Fortitude

2 Peter 1:6

Introduction:

The Greek word translated "patience" is a much stronger word than rendered here. It is active rather than passive. It is much more steadfast endurance.

I. **Patience Is Persistence of Purpose**
   A. Word has lost its meaning over centuries—become much less intense and strong
   B. Two words translated "patience"—both used in Col. 1:11 (KJV)
      1. "Longsuffering"—how we handle (difficult) people
      2. "Patience"—how we handle circumstances; it is hanging-in when things get tough (opposite of quitting, complaining, going sour)

II. **Patience Is Proof of Possession**
   A. Patience proves salvation (Luke 8:15)
      1. Continued fruit-bearing is proof of genuine conversion
      2. Caution: this is a relative concept
   B. Patience authenticates service (2 Cor. 6:4)
      1. Steadfast endurance shows that one is a servant
      2. Steadfast endurance shows that one is serving God

III. **Patience Is Part of the Process**
   A. What God is doing in your life (Rom. 5:3–4; 8:29–30); without patience, you'll miss steps in the Christian life
   B. Keeps us on the go for God (Heb. 12:1); patience keeps us running the race set before us without dropping out of the course
   C. Keeps us enduring until God's purposes are complete (James 1:2–12); trials have a purpose; endurance keeps us under them until they have accomplished their purpose

IV. **Patience Is a Product of Prayer**
   A. God is its source (Rom. 15:5)
      1. "Patience" (steadfast endurance) never used of God—He has no need of it as He orders circumstances

       2. "Patience" (long-suffering) frequently used of Him—He chooses to put up with people
- B. Prayer is its means (Col. 1:11)
  1. This is part of Paul's prayer for the Colossians
  2. Patience comes through prayerful seeking of it

V. Patience Is a Partner of Promises
We should have patience because:
- A. His promises are sure (Heb. 10:36)
  1. The only thing unsure about His promises is the timing of them
  2. Endurance keeps us around long enough to see them fulfilled
- B. Jesus is returning (1 Thess. 1:3; 2 Thess. 3:5)
  1. This world isn't all there is to it
  2. There is a designated end
- C. He will right all wrongs (James 5:1–11)
  1. This will happen at His coming
  2. Job an example of God righting wrongs
  3. Hang in there—He will straighten out all things when He comes

Conclusion:
We need a fresh view of God and his dealings with men if we are ever to develop patience. You can count on God!

Seeing the Unseen
2 Peter 1:6

Introduction:
Some people believe that we are gods. Others believe that we have God within us. The Bible teaches that we are to be godly. What does that mean?

I. **Its Definition**
   A. It is not to be god-like
      1. This is impossible without the divine nature
      2. It is not even adequate to be like what God wants us to be like
   B. It is a constant God-consciousness
      1. A constant awareness of God
      2. A continual consideration of God
   C. It is exemplified in Moses (Heb. 11:27): note the phrase, "as seeing Him who is invisible" (KJV)

II. **Its Details**
   A. Recognition of the existence of God (Heb. 11:6)
   B. Realization of the greatness of God (Ps. 50)
   C. Subordination to the authority of God
      1. Not voluntary placing oneself under another
      2. Actual recognition of the superiority of another
   D. Submission to the direction of God
      1. Doing what He says at all times
      2. Doing what He says at once, cheerfully and fully
   E. Tribute to the glory of God—a life lived to His glory
      1. Conversation
      2. Conduct
      3. Prayer
      4. Worship

III. **Its Direction**
   A. Doctrine
      1. All belief must take Him into account
      2. All we can know of Him is found in Scripture
      3. What we believe determines what we do
   B. Practice
      1. God-consciousness shows in action
      2. My conduct demonstrates my faith

IV. Its Demands

A. Negative
1. Should keep me from things that please Satan
2. Should keep me from things that displease God

B. Positive
1. Should motivate to right with great encouragement that it is worthwhile: we serve the Lord
2. Should motivate to steadfast endurance: God-consciousness will enable me to keep going in the tough times
3. Should motivate to increasing knowledge; we will want to know more about someone as fascinating as He

Conclusion:

Paul said, "Godliness . . . is great gain" (1 Tim. 6:6).

Philadelphia

2 Peter 1:7

Introduction:
"Brotherly kindness" is actually a poor translation. Much better would be to read "brotherly love." The words of an older folk song—"Then There Is Love"—form the words of an outline.

I. **Then There Is Love in General**
    A. Love defined: it involves emotion but is more than feeling
        1. It always involves action
        2. The action involved is always related to giving
        3. Love: action that gives someone what is needed on the deepest level of that need
    B. Love detailed
        1. It is commanded—something that can be learned and done
        2. It deals with relationships (Rom. 12:10; 1 Pet. 1:22)
        3. It is unconditional
        4. It is always under control

II. **Then There Is Love to the Brethren**
    A. It is commanded (John 13:34)
        1. A "new" commandment—more a new emphasis
        2. "That ye love one another"—emphasis on the family of faith
        3. "As I have loved you"—a pattern and a demand
    B. It is reasoned (1 John 4:20)
        1. If you can't love your brother whom you have seen . . .
        2. How can you love the God you have not seen?
    C. It is purposeful (John 13:35)
        1. It demonstrates obedience
        2. It demonstrates possession of His love
        3. It demonstrates likeness to Him

III. **Then There Is Love to All the Brethren**
    A. It is inclusive: it is sometimes easier to love the unsaved than to love the brethren
        1. Those whom we like and relate to
        2. Those whom we do not like

      3. Those who do not like us or treat us the way we think they should
  B. It is exclusive—in a very different way
      1. Rules out all limitations
      2. Eliminates all excuses
      3. Contains no conditions
  C. It is inclusive: our love for the brethren is the logical conclusion of His love for us
      1. If He loves them, who are we not to do so?
      2. If He loves us, why should we not love them?
      3. If He has commanded us, and we love Him. . . ?

Conclusion:

Let's get practical. Discover a need of another Christian and do something to meet it. Do something for someone who has been unkind, etc., to you.

Tough Love
2 Peter 1:7

Introduction:
To your basic faith add: Virtue—moral excellence; Knowledge—spiritual discernment; Temperance—self-control; Patience—steadfast endurance; Godliness—God consciousness; Brotherly kindness—love for the brethren. Now the more general term for love; the term usually used in conjunction with our love for God.

I. **Love for God Established (Deut. 6:5; Matt. 22:37; 12:29–30; Luke 10:27)**
   A. It must be prioritized—placed before any other love
      1. In time sequence
      2. In intensity
      3. In importance
   B. It must be pure
      1. Whole-hearted
      2. Without dilution
      3. Without reservation

II. **Love for God Explained**
   A. It is not
      1. Emotions—good and warm feelings stirred up toward God
      2. Expressions—words I speak about God
      3. Exercises—those religious acts that I do
      4. Efforts—good works that I do in the interest of God and His work
   B. It is
      1. Action
      2. Specific action
      3. Obedient action (John 14:15, 21–3; 15:10; 1 John 5:3)
         a. Complete obedience—all that it knows to do
         b. Curious obedience—wants to know all there is to know
         c. Creative obedience—looks for ways to obey in order to please

III. **Love for God Extended**
   A. Love for God involves love for man
      1. Part of love for God is love for man (Matt. 22:37; Luke 10:27)

61

2. Can't love God without loving man
B. Love for God reverses a common misunderstanding
   1. Commandments seem as gloomy, negative, burdensome
   2. Commandments—directions on how to show our love
C. Love for God is practical in nature
   1. Will seek to act toward man
   2. Will seek to meet man's needs
   3. Will seek to win men to Christ

Conclusion:

There is so much confusion about love for God: mere talk, strong feelings, rituals, observances, good works. But real love is obedience. Do you really love God? It is easier to say, "I love you, Lord," than it is to live that love.